YAS

11/02

W9-BAZ-945

TRIANGLE HISTORIES
★ ★ ★ ★ ★ ★ ★ ★ ★
THE REVOLUTIONARY WAR

# ABIGAIL ADAMS

## Kate Davis

BLACKBIRCH®
PRESS

THOMSON

GALE

San Diego • Detroit • New York • San Francisco • Cleveland
New Haven, Conn. • Waterville, Maine • London • Munich

© 2002 by Blackbirch Press™. Blackbirch Press™ is an imprint of The Gale Group, Inc., a division of Thomson Learning, Inc.

Blackbirch Press™ and Thomson Learning™ are trademarks used herein under license.

*For more information, contact*
The Gale Group, Inc.
27500 Drake Rd.
Farmington Hills, MI 48331-3535
Or you can visit our Internet site at http://www.gale.com

Photo credits: Cover, cover (inset), pages 5, 7, 10, 24, 41, 49, 54, 59, 62, 67, 78, 81, 87 © North Wind Picture Archives; pages 9, 45, 69, 89, 94 © Archiving Early America; pages 16, 29, 34, 37, 50, 63, 70, 76, 93 © historypictures.com; page 46 © Bettman/CORBIS; page 79 © Historical Picture Archive/CORBIS; page 83 © Gianni Dagli Orti/CORBIS

Pages 9, 21, 43, 44, 45, 51, 55, 58, 60, 63: Reprinted by permission of the publisher from THE ADAMS PAPERS: ADAMS FAMILY CORRESPONDENCE, VOLUME I ~ 1761–May 1776, edited by L.H. Butterfield, Cambridge, Mass.: The Belknap Press of Harvard University Press, Copyright ©1963 by the Massachusetts Historical Society. Pages 64, 65, 68: Reprinted by permission of the publisher from THE ADAMS PAPERS: ADAMS FAMILY CORRESPONDENCE, VOLUME II ~ June 1776–March 1778, edited by L.H. Butterfield, Cambridge, Mass.: The Belknap Press of Harvard University Press, Copyright ©1963 by the Massachusetts Historical Society. Pages 82, 85: Reprinted by permission of the publisher from THE ADAMS PAPERS: ADAMS FAMILY CORRESPONDENCE, VOLUME III ~ April 1778–September 1780, edited by L.H. Butterfield and Marc Friedlander, Cambridge, Mass.: The Belknap Press of Harvard University Press, Copyright ©1973 by the Massachusetts Historical Society. For Diary and Autobiography of John Adams: Reprinted by permission of the publisher from DIARY AND AUTOBIOGRAPHY OF JOHN ADAMS, Vols I–IV, edited by L.H. Butterfield, Cambridge, Mass.: The Belknap Press of Harvard University Press, Copyright ©1961 by the Massachusetts Historical Society. Quotations from the Adams Papers are from the microfilm edition, by permission of the Massachusetts Historical Society.

**LIBRARY OF CONGRESS CATALOGING-IN-PUBLICATION DATA**

Davis, Kate.
 Abigail Adams / by Kate Davis.
  p. cm. — (Triangle history of the American Revolution. Revolutionary War leaders)
 Summary: Profiles a woman who is remembered for her intellectual accomplishments, belief in women's rights, and support of her husband, John, who became the second president of the United States.
 Includes index.
 ISBN 1-56711-610-8 (hardback : alk. paper)
 1. Adams, Abigail, 1744-1818—Juvenile literature. 2. Presidents' spouses—United States—Biography—Juvenile literature. [1. Adams, Abigail, 1744-1818. 2. First ladies. 3. Women—Biography.] I. Title. II. Series.
 E322.1.A38 D38 2003
 973.4'4'092—dc21                                    2002003376

**Printed in China**
10 9 8 7 6 5 4 3 2 1

# CONTENTS

# PREFACE: THE AMERICAN REVOLUTION

Today, more than two centuries after the final shots were fired, the American Revolution remains an inspiring story not only to Americans, but also to people around the world. For many citizens, the well-known battles that occurred between 1775 and 1781—such as Lexington, Trenton, Yorktown, and others—represent the essence of the Revolution. In truth, however, the formation of the United States involved much more than the battles of the Revolutionary War. The creation of our nation occurred over several decades, beginning in 1763, at the end of the French and Indian War, and continuing until 1790, when the last of the original 13 colonies ratified the Constitution.

More than two hundred years later, it may be difficult to fully appreciate the courage and determination of the people who fought for, and founded, our nation. The decision to declare independence was not made easily—and it was not unanimous. Breaking away from England—the ancestral land of most colonists—was a bold and difficult move. In addition to the emotional hardship of revolt, colonists faced the greatest military and economic power in the world at the time.

The first step on the path to the Revolution was essentially a dispute over money. By 1763, England's treasury had been drained in order to pay for the French and Indian War. British lawmakers, as well as England's new ruler, King George III, felt that the colonies should help to pay for the war's expense and for the cost of housing the British troops who remained in the colonies. Thus began a series of oppressive British tax acts and other laws that angered the colonists and eventually provoked full-scale violence.

King George III

The Stamp Act of 1765 was followed by the Townshend
Acts in 1767. Gradually, colonists were forced to pay
taxes on dozens of everyday goods from playing cards to
paint to tea. At the same time, the colonists had no say in
the passage of these acts. The more colonists complained
that "taxation without representation is tyranny," the
more British lawmakers claimed the right to make laws

for the colonists "in all cases whatsoever." Soldiers and tax collectors were sent to the colonies to enforce the new laws. In addition, the colonists were forbidden to trade with any country but England.

Each act of Parliament pushed the colonies closer to unifying in opposition to English laws. Boycotts of British goods inspired protests and violence against tax collectors. Merchants who continued to trade with the Crown risked attacks by their colonial neighbors. The rising violence soon led to riots against British troops stationed in the colonies and the organized destruction of British goods. Tossing tea into Boston Harbor was just one destructive act. That event, the Boston Tea Party, led England to pass the so-called Intolerable Acts of 1774. The port of Boston was closed, more British troops were sent to the colonies, and many more legal rights for colonists were suspended.

Finally, there was no turning back. Early on an April morning in 1775, at Lexington Green in Massachusetts, the first shots of the American Revolution were fired. Even after the first battle, the idea of a war against England seemed unimaginable to all but a few radicals. Many colonists held out hope that a compromise could be reached. Except for the Battle of Bunker Hill and some minor battles at sea, the war ceased for much of 1775. During this time, delegates to the Continental Congress struggled to reach a consensus about the next step.

During those uncertain months, the Revolution was fought, not on a military battlefield, but on the battlefield of public opinion. Ardent rebels—especially Samuel Adams and Thomas Paine—worked tirelessly to keep the spirit of revolution alive. They stoked the fires of revolt by writing letters and pamphlets, speaking at public gatherings, organizing boycotts, and devising other forms of protest. It was their brave efforts that kept others focused on liberty and freedom until July 4, 1776. On that day, Thomas Jefferson's Declaration of Independence left no doubt about the intentions of the colonies. As John Adams wrote afterward, the "revolution began in hearts and minds not on the battlefield."

As unifying as Jefferson's words were, the United States did not become a nation the moment the Declaration of Independence claimed the right of all people to "life, liberty, and the pursuit of happiness." Before, during, and after the war, Americans who spoke of their "country" still generally meant whatever colony was their home. Some colonies even had their own navies during the war, and a few sent their own representatives to Europe to seek aid for their colony alone while delegates from the Continental Congress were doing the same job for the whole United States. Real national unity did not begin to take hold until the inauguration of George Washington in 1789, and did not fully bloom until the dawn of the 19th century.

The story of the American Revolution has been told for more than two centuries and may well be told for centuries to come. It is a tribute to the men and women who came together during this unique era that, to this day, people the world over find inspiration in the story of the Revolution. In the words of the Declaration of Independence, these great Americans risked "their lives, their fortunes, and their sacred honor" for freedom.

The Minuteman statue stands in Concord, Massachusetts.

# Introduction:
# "The Decisive Day
# Is Come"

Thunder in the distance woke Abigail Adams hours before dawn on June 17, 1775. Half asleep, she thought an earthquake, like one she had lived through as a little girl, was shaking the farmhouse.

As morning light seeped through the shuttered windows of her home in Braintree, Massachusetts, Adams realized that the booming sounds came from cannons. Adams rose, said a prayer, dressed quickly, and made a fire to prepare breakfast for her four young children. Her husband, John Adams, was far away in Philadelphia, where he served as a delegate to the Second Continental Congress. Representatives from the colonies were meeting there to debate a course of action against British rule.

Like other colonists—especially those in Massachusetts—Abigail Adams had been expecting a battle like the one she heard to the north. In April, there had been a skirmish between colonists and British soldiers in Lexington. The battle had continued in Concord, and the British redcoats were forced to retreat to Boston with heavy losses.

As the sun rose on June 17, Adams took her oldest son, John Quincy, by the hand and climbed Penn's Hill near the family's home. Looking north, she saw that Charlestown, across the harbor from Boston, was on fire. Black smoke billowed into the

The Battle of Bunker Hill was costly for both the British and the colonists.

sky as cannons from huge British warships pounded the American forces camped near Bunker Hill.

Kneeling by her son, she asked him to recite a poem she had taught him to honor the men who fought: "How sleep the brave, who sink to rest/ By all their country's wishes blest!" Then the mother and son walked home.

Throughout the day in Charlestown, colonists and redcoats remained locked in a bloody battle near Bunker Hill. The battle, later named for Bunker Hill but actually fought on nearby Breed's Hill, ended only when the colonists ran out of gunpowder and fled. Before they retreated, they had killed nearly 1,000 British troops, and lost about 400 of their own men.

Adams, before her husband had left, had expressed the hope that the colonists could win their freedom from England without violence. As the sun set on June 17, however, she wrote one of her frequent letters to her husband. Among the words she wrote to him that day were: "The decisive Day is come on which the fate of America depends."

9

# Chapter 1

## INDEPENDENT
## MIND AND SPIRIT

Today, nearly 200 years after her death, the
girl born Abigail Smith, who grew up to become
known as Abigail Adams, is one of the most
respected women of early America. Her lifelong
correspondence with her husband and other
notable people provides one of the clearest pictures
of life during the time of the American Revolution.

OPPOSITE: Abigail Adams was a person of strong will and firm opinions.

Adams was unique in her determination to develop and speak her mind at a time when many young women grew up illiterate and ignored. Adams's inner strength showed not only in her intellectual achievements, but in her ability to take care of her farm and family alone during the many years when her husband was away in service to the cause of independence.

## Virtue First

Abigail Smith was born on November 11, 1744, the second of four children, to William Smith and Elizabeth Quincy. Elizabeth was descended from the first settlers of the Massachusetts Bay Colony. William was the parson of the Congregational Church in Weymouth, a seacoast village south of Boston. He was a graduate of Harvard College and the son of a successful merchant. Invited to become the president of Harvard, he chose instead to become a minister. Like many preachers of his day, Reverend Smith was also a farmer. He tended an apple orchard and cornfields, and grew crops of carrots, potatoes, squash, and barley. Cows and sheep were the family's livestock.

★

In 1744, Samuel Adams was fired from his first job as a bookkeeper.

★

As a girl, Abigail was sickly. Her mother was cautious about her daughter's health, with good reason. Though herbal remedies were available, few medicines had been developed because colonists knew little about the causes of illness. Disease spread quickly through villages. In 1751, eleven children in Weymouth died of diphtheria, a contagious throat disease, in one week alone.

Elizabeth Smith would not allow her frail daughter to attend the small primary schools that existed in Massachusetts at that time, but William firmly believed that girls should be educated. With her father, her sister Mary, and her grandmother Quincy as tutors, Abigail learned to read and write well at a young age. Her spelling remained poor throughout her life—a common problem even among educated people of that time.

For the Smiths, the most important lesson they wanted their children to learn was the principle of virtue. William taught Abigail to speak only of the positive qualities of people. Abigail's mother refused to gossip or quarrel. As a minister's wife, she often visited the sick and helped the poor. "Never wait to be requested to do a kind office, an act of love," she told her children. Abigail accompanied her mother on these visits, practicing charity wherever it was needed.

## Daily Life

Abigail's childhood, like that of most girls in colonial times, was filled with domestic chores. Most people grew their own food and built their own homes. Preparing meals took a large part of each day. Although the Smiths had hired help, Abigail and her sisters, Mary and Betsy, still learned to make cooking fires, bake bread in a wall oven, and work the heavy black kettles that hung

13

from hooks over the hearth. Abigail churned butter, shucked corn, and shelled peas.

Elizabeth Smith trained her daughters how clean and spin wool as well as how to weave, stitch, and mend. The girls made soap and candles and grew an herb garden—all skills required to manage a household. Abigail also loved to tend lambs in the barn.

Although busy with her education and chores, Abigail was curious about the goings-on in her town. She often asked to go into Weymouth. Young ladies were not allowed to go wherever they pleased, her mother said. Nor did girls "run, jump, skip, or show emotions." Elizabeth Smith worried that Abigail, her middle daughter, was becoming unmanageable as she grew into her teenage years. Grandmother Quincy disagreed. She doted on Abigail. "Wild colts make the best horses," Grandmother Quincy said.

## Sharpening Her Mind

Elizabeth Smith's parents owned a stately home called Mount Wollaston. It overlooked Boston Harbor in Braintree. Abigail often went there to recover when she was ill, and while the fresh seas breezes restored her body, the huge library of her grandfather, John Quincy, nourished her mind. As she grew up, Abigail read every book she could get her hands on.

Church also expanded Abigail's mind. Worship was at the center of most colonists' lives. William

Smith's Congregational Church was more open-minded than many Puritan churches, the more rigid branch of their Protestant faith. Puritans were taught that humans were sinful and that God saved only an elect few. Smith, on the other hand, preached that faith and moral conduct were essential. He also believed that people could decide many spiritual matters for themselves and should not be bound by strict doctrines.

Smith's beliefs were similar to those of a small but growing number of ministers in the Massachusetts Bay Colony who preached that freedom was God's reward for a life of virtue. As Abigail became more aware of the world around her, her father's teachings helped shape her desire for both personal and political freedom.

## Broadening the Circle

Her home environment deepened Abigail's understanding of religious thought and political issues. Her father sometimes allowed her a rare privilege for young women of her day—to listen in when he held meetings with leaders of the Weymouth church. She wanted to participate, but was not allowed to speak to the deacons or question them. Even more than she wanted to speak with adults, Abigail longed to discuss news, books, and fashions with other young people. She had few peers at home in tiny Weymouth, however, to whom she could turn for thought-provoking fellowship.

15

Abigail Adams

In the mid-1700s, Boston was one of the busiest and most important ports in the colonies.

Abigail Adams

Abigail was able to find other ways to keep her mind active, though. She and Mary were permitted to visit Uncle Isaac and Aunt Elizabeth Smith in the bustling city of Boston. Isaac was a wealthy merchant. The Smiths owned a mansion with large rooms, crystal chandeliers, beautiful furniture, and many servants. Abigail spent long hours in Isaac's library, which held far more volumes than her grandfather's library.

Isaac's home was also a gathering place for young people in Boston. Abigail's cousin, Isaac Jr., and his friends often studied together there for the entrance examination to Harvard, one of the nation's first and finest colleges, located in Cambridge across the Charles River from Boston. Abigail longed to further her own education, but because she had no formal schooling, no knowledge of Latin, and, most of all, because she was a girl, she had no chance of going to college.

With Isaac Jr. and his friends, however, Abigail joined lively discussions of literature and world affairs. The young people talked about English poetry. They debated whether their colony could protect itself from French invaders without England's navy. Abigail befriended other young women who also gathered for discussions while the boys studied. They included Eunice Paine, Mary Nicholson, and Polly Palmer, all of whom became lifelong friends. When she returned to her quiet farmhouse, Abigail corresponded with them and with her cousin Isaac.

# Literary Leanings

Abigail soon realized that almost nothing gave her greater pleasure than putting her thoughts down on paper. Few women of the mid-1700s expected to become professional writers. Even if they had the ability, there were no opportunities for women. Writing letters was one of the only acceptable ways a woman could express her thoughts. As a teenager, Abigail took advantage of this way to exercise her mind. She wrote letters constantly. In them, she shared what she learned in her reading and exchanged ideas with her friends.

Writing letters also allowed Abigail to use her imagination. She and her friends adopted pen names. Abigail called herself Diana, after the Roman goddess of the hunt and the moon. She developed her own literary style, which she learned in part from reading English magazines. Her writing became more poetic after Abigail met an English gentleman named Richard Cranch. Cranch was courting Abigail's older sister, Mary. He enjoyed reading the works of William Shakespeare and poets such as John Milton and Alexander Pope to the Smith sisters. Abigail memorized many verses and poems.

As Abigail matured, she became aware that if she did not marry, she would be financially dependent on her family. There were few ways at that time for women to earn their own way in the world. Although she believed that a woman's highest duty was to fulfill the role of wife and mother, she also knew that when she married she would give up her legal rights. The challenge would be to find a husband who would support and encourage her restless mind.

## "Partner of All My Joys"

When Richard Cranch came to visit Mary Smith, he sometimes brought along a bright young lawyer named John Adams. Abigail had first met John in 1759, when she was 15, but she had been unimpressed with the young man, who was nine years older than she was. Overweight and overly talkative, John Adams had come across as arrogant. To John, Abigail seemed to be "lacking in tenderness." Even so, John returned often, since interesting conversation was part of daily life in the Smith household.

John Adams was born in 1735 and educated at Harvard College. He graduated in 1755. His first job was as a teacher, but he found the job unsatisfying and decided to study law. In 1758, he started his own practice in Braintree, only 4 miles from Weymouth.

By the time Abigail turned 17, John Adams had begun to appreciate her quick wit, piercing dark eyes, and constant curiosity. Abigail herself had come to admire John's ambition and sense of humor. Adams knew how to make the Smith sisters laugh. He freely shared his ideas—sometimes too freely. Abigail was a good listener, but she did not hesitate to speak out when Adams seemed too full of himself. Adams, who kept a journal throughout his life, confessed that he had never met a woman like Abigail. Before long, they were courting.

Abigail's father was agreeable to the romance, but his wife was not pleased. John did not come from a wealthy family. His father was a farmer and shoemaker. As a member of the prominent Quincy family, Elizabeth Smith had expected her daughter to marry someone from a similar background. Family was not the only issue standing in the way, either. John Adams was a lawyer, and lawyers were not highly respected. Despite Elizabeth's objections, however, there was no denying John's intelligence. He was also a landowner, since he had inherited a house when his father died. Even though she had reservations, Elizabeth ultimately agreed to permit the courtship.

By 1762, Abigail and John Adams were writing frank and affectionate letters to each other. John addressed his letters to "Miss Adorable." He described Abigail as "Tender...sensible, friendly...Prudent, modest, delicate, soft ...obliging, active." John was quite willing to express his feelings. He wrote: "The dear Partner of all my Joys and sorrow, in whose Affections, and Friendship I glory, ...comes into my Mind very often and makes me sigh." In her letters, Abigail called John "my dearest friend" and said they were "cast in the same mould."

★

In 1762, Lord Charles Cornwallis took a seat in the British Parliament.

★

21

The two quickly realized they were in love and decided to marry. John wanted to become financially stable, however, so they waited a while before the wedding. A smallpox epidemic in Boston delayed their plans in late 1763. They spent the summer of 1764 preparing for the wedding, but then Abigail fell ill with a fever. Finally, on October 25, 1764, they were married in Weymouth by Abigail's father.

John Adams was a lawyer when he and Abigail first met.

The Adamses moved into John's modest home, a short walk from his mother's house. John turned the kitchen into a law office. When he was not traveling to see clients in Boston, he farmed the land and managed a woodlot with hired help.

Abigail had a servant who helped her with the cooking and cleaning, but she did much of the housework herself. Her days were filled with sewing, cooking, and baking. She also tended the vegetable garden and looked after the livestock.

Working the farm was a full-time job, but the young couple enjoyed their time together. They were happy with simple pleasures such as walks up Penn's Hill when time allowed. They also spent time reading together and discussing political affairs. Abigail was very happy in her new life.

# Chapter 2

## REVOLUTIONARY RUMBLINGS

In her first year of marriage, the young Mrs. Adams gave birth to a baby girl. The baby was named Abigail, but was affectionately called "Nabby." The new father could not wait to return from crowded, noisy Boston to his wife and daughter and the Braintree farm. The new family, however, would not be able to enjoy their quiet home for long.

OPPOSITE: The French and Indian War caused the British government to fall deeply into debt—and to tax the colonies to repay that debt.

## Unfair Trade Laws

By 1765, Massachusetts had been a corporate
colony of the English Crown for almost 75 years.
This meant that colonists were permitted to choose
their own governor and elect their own assemblies
of representatives. Massachusetts was founded by
men and women who had been turned away from
the royal Church of England because of their faith.
Thus, the people had never been especially loyal to
royalty. Separated from England by an ocean, they
had developed an independent spirit. For many
years, the rulers in England had ignored that
independence. The hands-off policy changed,
however, when King George III came to the throne
in 1760 at the age of 22.

By the mid-1760s, George III had pushed British
Parliament to convert all of America to royal
colonies. This allowed him to abolish any colonial
assemblies and appoint his own governors. Most
colonies, especially those that provided great
wealth to the Crown, like Virginia, were already
royal colonies. Before the 1760s, the king had
cared little about New England economically.
Its cool climate, harbors that were ice-choked in
winter, and rocky soil made it unfit to raise cash
crops such as tobacco and cotton that could be
shipped to England for sale.

Events in the colonies and abroad, however,
changed the relationship between England and
America. In 1763, England had finally defeated

France in the Seven Years' War, known in the colonies as the French and Indian War. The British had taken control of Canada and territories east of the Mississippi River from France. It was a costly victory: England was left millions of pounds in debt and had nowhere to turn for more money. The English people were already overburdened with taxes. British lawmakers and George III agreed that the colonies should pay for the protection they received from the British.

By 1765, England had decided to raise the money it needed from Massachusetts and all the other American colonies through taxation and duties—taxes on imported goods. Parliament first passed the Sugar Act. This law forced colonists to pay a duty on any sugar that came into the colonies from places other than the British West Indies. It was the first of several acts that forced colonists to buy only British goods.

Next, American merchants felt the weight of British trade and navigation laws. These regulated markets and prices for raw materials produced in the colonies. The result was that England could set the prices for American goods— and force Americans to sell only to the British.

Boston merchants, like Abigail's uncle Isaac, complained that their ships were not allowed to sell colonial woolen goods anywhere in the world or to transport barrel staves to wine-producing Portugal, for example. The restrictions also had a direct effect on the price of wool that small-scale farmers such as the Adamses could earn from their sheep.

## The Stamp Act

In 1765, England's Parliament imposed the Stamp Act on the colonies. All legal documents—deeds, licenses, court papers, diplomas, wills, even playing cards—were required to bear official stamps, which had to be bought when the items were purchased. The fees for the stamps were used to pay down England's war debt.

The colonists saw the stamps for exactly what they were—taxes. After years of making their own laws and rules, colonists were not willing to pay duties to England, which they now saw as a foreign power. The colonists of Massachusetts did more than simply refuse to pay the duties, however. They attacked and beat British tax collectors and destroyed the offices of any merchants who imported taxable British goods.

Without stamps, business came to a standstill in Boston and the surrounding areas. Courts were closed, and John Adams—the lawyer—was out of work. The financial pinch forced the Adamses to rely on what they could raise on their small farm to support them.

In the evenings, Abigail and John discussed the colony's dilemma. The stamps themselves were not very costly, but they represented a loss of liberty. If the British could tax paper, the Adamses wondered, what would they tax next?

Colonial newspapers printed protests such as this against the hated Stamp Act.

John Adams expressed his views on the subject in political essays that were published in the *Boston Gazette*. "The world may know," he wrote, "in present and all future generations... that we never can be slaves." He also attended political gatherings in Boston with his older cousin, Samuel Adams, a fiery rebel who had formed an anti-tax group called the Sons of Liberty to protest the Stamp Act. Speakers at these events urged colonists to fight "taxation without representation."

As a result of his essays and his presence at the rallies, John was selected with a committee of other men to petition Massachusetts governor Francis Bernard for repeal of the Stamp Act. As a result of those protests and others throughout the colonies, the British Parliament repealed the law in 1766. Boston colonists celebrated the repeal with cannons, churchbells, and drums. John celebrated by resuming his legal practice.

## Women's Role and Refinement

John's writing in the Boston newspaper had gained notice. He was soon in great demand as a lawyer. Because lawyers of his time had to travel to argue cases, he was often gone from home. His practice took him on the New England court circuit, north to Maine and southeast to Cape Cod. Abigail missed her husband a great deal. She had his books to keep her company, but she was lonely for his cheerful conversation. She also had to handle many of the daily farming chores by herself.

Abigail's mother, by that time in ill health, was unable to see or help her daughter. Adams longed for the company of her older sister, but Mary had moved to Salem, north of Boston—a long trip in those days. By February 1767, Adams missed

Mary's thoughts and advice on childrearing especially, because she was pregnant again.

Adams took her family responsibilities seriously. She read James Fordyce's popular book, *Sermons to Young Women.* In it, the author reminded women that their purpose in life was not only to be helpmates to the men who supported them, but also to be guardians of religion and virtue. Women were responsible for the personal development of their children, Fordyce wrote. It was up to mothers to nurture and encourage the proper growth of children. By doing so, he wrote, women could make a valuable contribution to society.

Although Fordyce believed that women's place was in the home, he pushed the boundaries of that traditional view. He urged women to read history, biography, literature, and travel books. He also wrote that they should learn household economics and practice the arts.

The more she read, the more Adams—now age twenty-three—questioned what role she and other women could play in a changing political environment. Many questions that she asked herself in her own personal search were echoed in the questions colonists asked about their role as subjects of the British Crown.

## The Townshend Act

In 1766, when the British repealed the Stamp Act, Parliament passed the Declaratory Act, which gave England the right to pass laws and tax the colonies "in all cases whatsoever." It was Parliament's way of saving its self-respect. This act united the colonists. In response to the Declaratory Act, a congress of colonial leaders met in New York and declared that only the colonies could levy taxes in America. In one speech, delegate Christopher Gadsden stated that, "There ought to be no more New England men, no New Yorkers ... but all of us Americans!"

When England passed a new set of tax laws in 1767—the Townshend Acts—it weakened even further any remaining colonial allegiance to the Crown. The Townshend Acts called for steep duties on items such as paint, glass, lead, paper, and tea. The colonists were outraged and vowed to boycott British goods.

Adams realized that the daily choices she made had political effects. She refused to buy tea and she made her own linen rather than buy English cloth. During this time of patriotic defiance, Adams gave birth to her second child, a boy, on July 11, 1767. She named him John Quincy, after her beloved grandfather, who had recently died.

## Tensions Mount

As a popular spokesman for the liberty movement, John Adams was expected to be present at political clubs and coffeehouse discussions. He spent more evenings in the city and fewer at home. Thus, in April 1768, when John asked Abigail if she would move the family into Boston, she did not hesitate.

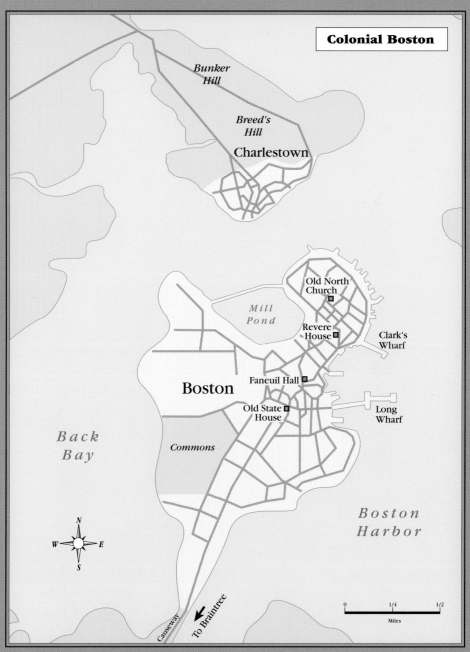

**Colonial Boston**

Bunker
Hill

Breed's
Hill

Charlestown

Old North
Church

Mill
Pond

Revere
House

Clark's
Wharf

Faneuil Hall

Boston

Old State
House

Long
Wharf

Back
Bay

Commons

Boston
Harbor

N
W   E
S

Causeway

To Braintree

0     1/4     1/2

Miles

Colonial Boston was built on a peninsula.

Faneuil Hall was the main marketplace in colonial Boston.

Her sister Mary and Richard Cranch had already moved there. Her aunt, uncle, and cousin lived in the city as well. Now that Abigail had two children

to raise, she longed to be close to family members with whom she shared a special bond.

Boston was a bustling port city of about 16,000 people in 1768. The Adamses rented a house on Brattle Square, just steps from Town Hall and its courts, and two blocks from Faneuil Hall—the Boston market and meeting place. It was a short walk to the city green, called the common, as well as wharves and shops.

The Adamses attended the Brattle Street Congregational Church, and Abigail entertained John's influential friends in their home. She was an engaging presence at her husband's side. She read the newspapers and easily took part in political discussions. She became a good friend of Samuel Adams's wife, Betsy, and of physician Joseph Warren, who cared for her children. Living in Boston also allowed Abigail to hear John argue a case for the first time.

Although Abigail was stirred by the atmosphere of the city, Boston was growing uneasier by the day. Opposition to the Townshend Acts had become more brutal than the fight against the Stamp Act. Furious colonists "tarred and feathered" any merchant or official who did not support the boycott of British goods. This was no childish prank. It was a harsh torture. Boiling-hot tar was poured on the person's naked body, which burned the skin severely. Down and feathers were dumped over the hot, sticky tar. Then the person was forced to leave town.

Tensions finally boiled over when a British customs agent tried to collect taxes on wealthy John Hancock's ship *Liberty*. A mob beat the agent, which led the British to send a fleet of warships to Boston Harbor. England posted more troops in red coats to protect British officials in Boston. Some of these troops drilled right outside the Adamses' windows. The sound of fifes, drums, and soldiers clattering on the cobblestones woke the family every day.

Just after Christmas 1768, Abigail Adams gave birth to a third child, Susanna, who was small and sickly. With all the commotion in the streets,

36

A tax collector is tarred and feathered in a political cartoon of the time.

neither the baby nor the mother got much sleep, even after the family moved twice.

Dr. Joseph Warren visited the household to tend ailments, and he sometimes lingered to discuss politics with John. Medicine of the day was not enough to save the Adamses' daughter. Little Susanna died in February 1770, shortly after her first birthday.

37

## A Defense of Justice

By that time, British troops quartered in Boston had taken over Faneuil Hall and part of the State House. Bostonians detested this intrusion. Young men taunted the soldiers. They flung debris at them and called the soldiers "lobsterbacks" because of their red coats. Many redcoats were convicts or men who had failed at everything else in life. They earned just two cents a day, out of which uniform expenses were deducted. They had to spend hours to groom and dress themselves in tight, itchy wool uniforms. They seldom had the luxury of bathing and were whipped for the slightest infraction.

In early March 1770, the mood in the streets of Boston was dangerous. So when John Adams heard alarms ring out one night, he raced home from a club meeting in dread. Abigail, still mourning Susanna's death, was pregnant with a fourth child, and John feared for his family's safety.

When John arrived home, he learned that a fight had broken out between a mob of colonists and a much smaller group of redcoats. The soldiers felt threatened and opened fire, killing five men in what became known as the Boston Massacre. John's family was safe, but blood had been shed. The next day Bostonians demanded that the British captain and his soldiers be tried for murder.

Of all of Boston's lawyers, only John seemed to care if the soldiers received a fair trial. When he

# The Boston Massacre

The skirmish that became known as the Boston Massacre took place on March 5, 1770. It began simply enough. A teenage boy had chased after a British officer near the Customs House and accused the captain of not paying a shop bill. A sentry posted nearby overheard and came to the officer's defense. The boy insulted the sentry, who quickly knocked him down with the butt of this rifle.

The boy fled but then returned with an angry gang. The mob swelled to include men from the docks brandishing clubs. Soon after the captain called for backup, a squad of British soldiers arrived to repel the seething crowd. Tempers flared; curses flew, and with them, rocks.

Through the shouts and dares, the confused redcoats thought they heard orders to shoot. In chaos and fear, they opened fire on the mob. When it was over, five colonists lay dead or dying in the mud and snow.

was asked to serve as defense lawyer, he agreed, even though he knew that the decision would make him unpopular. The colonies would not be governed by mobs, he vowed.

Adams agreed with her husband's decision. She saw a side of him that made him stand apart from those who were caught up in day-to-day political issues. John conducted himself with the stature of a statesman and a visionary.

John won the case in the fall of 1770. The jury found that the British captain and his men had fired in self-defense. Any fears for John's reputation vanished when he was asked to serve in the Massachusetts legislature.

Adams was worried about John's new assignment. She had a new baby—Charles, who had been born on May 29—and she knew John's duties would keep him away from home. He would also be unable to practice law while he was away. With a smaller law practice, there would be less money. Even worse, the British considered the legislature illegal. If John served, England could try him for treason.

Still, both Adamses had reached a point in their lives where a sense of duty to the cause of freedom was greater than their fear. John accepted the position and wrote in his journal that Abigail "was very sensible of all the Danger to her and to our Children as well as to me, but she thought I had done as I ought, she was very willing to share in all that was to come."

## Intolerable Acts

Over the next year, John's health suffered from the pressures of political obligations, his farm and law practice, and the need to support a family. In late 1771, vowing to "forsake politicks," he moved the family back to Braintree, but kept a small office in Boston.

Meanwhile, Abigail Adams was consumed with the day-to-day labor of raising children. In 1772, she had another son, Thomas. Soon, John's health was restored, but he wearied of the horseback commute to Boston and the time away from his family. Once again, the Adamses returned to Boston. As before, their timing coincided with rebellion there.

In 1773, the British East India Company had an oversupply of tea to sell, but did not have the money to pay the import taxes in England. Parliament wanted to help the company and make money as well. The lawmakers decided to let the company sell the tea to the colonists without requiring it to pay any import duty. The money would be made up by the duty the colonists had to pay to buy the tea. The colonists would benefit, according to British reasoning, because the company's tea would be cheaper than the tea they had been smuggling in.

Hoping to unload its tea in America, the British East India Company sent its cargo to Boston, but the company's plans did not work out as it had hoped. Many American merchants agreed to

41

boycott the tea, which Abigail Adams called "that bainful weed." To prevent the British from selling the tea to merchants who would not boycott, a group of men dressed like Mohawk Indians boarded the British tea ships on the night of December 16 and dumped 342 chests of tea into Boston Harbor.

★

In 1773, British officials stripped Thomas Paine of his job as a tax collector in England.

★

Furious, King George III retaliated. Parliament passed a series of laws that became known in the colonies as the Intolerable Acts. The Crown completely closed the port of Boston and promised that an army would soon arrive to enforce the closure. England also abolished town meetings in the colonies.

Adams feared that war was inevitable. She wrote to a friend, "The flame is kindled and like Lightning it catches from soul to soul. . . . Altho the mind is shocked at the Thought of sheding Humane Blood . . . if once they are made desperate Many, very Many of our Heroes will spend their lives in the cause."

## Correspondent at Home and Abroad

Adams had recently become acquainted with Mercy Warren, wife of one of John's political associates. Although few women were writers in her day, Warren had managed to publish plays under a male pen name. Her works were satires of political issues.

Adams often went to Plymouth with John to meet Mercy. Her husband was the brother of their

The Boston Tea Party in 1773 pushed the colonies and the British government closer to confrontation.

doctor, Joseph Warren, and it was in the Warrens' home that the Massachusetts Committee of Correspondence was formed. Each colony had a committee of correspondence that wrote reports to keep other colonies informed of events. Messages were delivered on horseback by swift post riders, such as Paul Revere. The groups helped greatly to unify the colonists at a time when news usually took months to pass from colony to colony.

Adams and Mercy Warren soon began their own correspondence. Warren valued the encouragement the Adamses gave her in regard to her writing. Abigail Adams sought Warren's advice on child-rearing and soon began to voice her political views as well. Warren and Adams fueled each other's expression and commitment to liberty. They agreed that virtuous people had to be on guard against corrupt power. People had certain rights that no one could take away. If a king violated those rights, his subjects could resist, Adams and Warren agreed.

Adams also became interested during this time in the work of another female writer, an English historian named Catherine Macaulay. An outspoken anti-royalty radical, Macaulay felt democratic reform could and should take place in America. John Adams had introduced Mercy and Abigail to Macaulay's writings so they could learn another woman's views. Abigail Adams felt so strongly about the work that she wrote to Macaulay as "one of my own Sex so eminent." In September 1774, she wrote:

44

*We are invaded with fleets and Armies, our commerce not only obstructed, but totally ruined, the courts of Justice shut, many driven out from the Metropolis, thousands reduced to want, or dependent upon the charity of their neighbors for a daily supply of food, all the Horrours of a civil war threatening us on one hand, and the chains of Slavery ready forged for us on the other.*

Adams supplied Macaulay with reports of the situation in America, as a foreign news correspondent might. In late 1774, she wrote, "The only alternative which every American thinks of is Liberty or Death." The following March, Patrick Henry echoed that phrase in a now-famous speech before the Virginia legislature, in which he said, "Give me liberty or give me death!"

Patrick Henry was a fiery speaker who strongly supported independence.

45

# Chapter 3

## "ON THE STAGE OF ACTION"

Abigail Adams lived through two kinds of revolutions. One was a struggle for survival under British oppression on the home front in Boston. The other took place on a larger stage. With her husband as a key player in the formation of a new government, Adams's thoughts turned often to the revolutionary task of creating a nation unlike any that had ever existed. "If we separate from Britain," she wrote to her husband, "what Code of Laws will be established?"

OPPOSITE: Untrained colonists at Bunker Hill found themselves face-to-face with the most powerful army in the world.

To separate from the Crown would require military force. Forming a new government would require wisdom. John Adams was called to address both requirements, and his wife's thoughts were among his most valuable guides.

## Buildup to Battle

In 1774, when word spread to the colonies that the British had closed the port of Boston, food and supplies were shipped overland to help those who suffered from the blockade. When the Crown removed the Massachusetts civil governor and appointed a military governor to replace him, the other colonists wondered how long it would be before England interfered with their governments, too. Revolution was in the air.

In Virginia, the colony's legislative branch, the House of Burgesses, refused to disband when England ordered it to do so as punishment for aiding Boston. Instead, in the summer of 1774, the representatives called for a Continental Congress in Philadelphia to address the colonies' plight. John Adams, together with John Hancock, Samuel Adams, and two other men, were elected to represent Massachusetts at that meeting.

John asked for his wife's support. He wrote to her from a circuit-court trip: "I must entreat you, my dear Partner... to take a Part with me in the Struggle." Adams feared the British would arrest John. To participate in a congress was treason to the Crown. On the other hand, she had read

Colonists in Boston hated the presence of British "lobsterbacks" in their city.

Philadelphia was the most important city in the colonies.

enough history to know that peace could not last without justice and liberty. She also knew the colonies needed a man like her husband.

Before he left for Philadelphia, John moved his family back to the safety of Braintree. All over Boston, signs of an impending conflict could be seen. The British had sent in 4,000 more troops. They had raided American ammunition supplies, dispersed angry crowds, and set up cannons on Beacon Hill, overlooking the city.

When John left for Philadelphia in August 1774, preparations for war had begun in outlying towns. Patriots trained as soldiers. Troops drilled in the streets, gunpowder supplies were secured, and

muskets and balls were made ready. Adams, alone with her children, feared what was to come. War could begin at any time, she knew. "Rocks and quick Sands appear upon every side," she wrote to John. Then, not wanting to distract him from his momentous task, she wished him wisdom in his work "upon the Stage of Action."

## Separation

Adams had her own busy stage of action at home. Unable to contact her husband with daily matters, she made decisions about the farm and family. She hired workers, decided when to harvest crops, and arranged to have John Quincy tutored.

51

In Philadelphia, John Adams was well known among colonial leaders and treated to lavish receptions, but he soon grew "wearied to death" of the tedious speeches of his fellow delegates. He said he would rather "Eat Potatoes and drink Water." With little or no income, he was concerned about his family at home. He need not have worried. Abigail Adams believed firmly in simplicity and she avoided showy display. To her, frugality was equal to virtue, and virtue was strength.

John returned home from the First Continental Congress in November 1774. Before they left, the delegates had agreed to meet in a second congress in the spring of 1775. In April, however, shortly before John and the other delegates departed for Philadelphia, an event occurred that firmly put Massachusetts and the other colonies on the road to revolution.

## Discord in Concord

Word had reached British governor Thomas Gage of Massachusetts that American rebels were hoarding ammunition in Concord, west of Boston. He was ordered by the Crown to seize it and to capture rebel leaders Samuel Adams and John Hancock at their lodgings in Lexington, where they were preparing to leave for the second congress.

The British troops marched silently out of Boston late on the night of April 18, 1775. They headed northwest. The colonists had spies everywhere, however, and the soldiers' movement was detected. Dr. Joseph Warren alerted Paul Revere and William Dawes to rally the militia—groups of citizen-soldiers. The riders traveled swiftly by horseback to warn the minutemen—Patriot soldiers who said they could be ready for duty at a moment's notice—that the British were coming.

In Lexington, before dawn on April 19, the British redcoats met unexpected resistance. At Lexington Green, colonial militia took on the most powerful army in the world. After a brief exchange of fire, eight Americans lay dead. To this day, no one knows who fired first—but the shots marked the official start of the American Revolution.

Although John Hancock and Samuel Adams had fled, the confident British pushed on to Concord and began to confiscate gunpowder supplies. For a while, the colonials watched helplessly as the British marched into town. When the redcoats set fire to the town hall, however, it enraged the militia gathered there. The colonists opened fire at redcoats stationed at the North Bridge in Concord. The redcoats, shocked to realize that they were under attack by a mob of angry farmers, fell back.

In the spring of 1775, Scottish immigrant John Paul Jones left Virginia for Philadelphia to seek a commission in the newly formed Continental navy.

The retreating British troops were met on the road back to Lexington by nearly 1,500 colonial soldiers who had answered the alarms in neighboring towns. The British soldiers were outnumbered and unprepared for the rebels' untraditional style of firing from behind trees and boulders. Close to

The retreat from Concord was a bloody defeat for the British.

Lexington, the redcoats broke ranks and fled. By the time they got back to Boston, 73 British were dead and more than 200 wounded. The Americans had lost 49, but John Hancock and Samuel Adams were safe. War was no longer on the horizon— it had arrived.

## Confusion and Courage

With Boston now a British stronghold, people loyal to the Crown swarmed into the city as anti-British colonists tried to leave. Each day, only a few people were allowed to leave, some with nothing but their

children and the clothes on their backs. Abigail Adams fed and housed some refugees in her farmhouse. Others desperately sought space to stay in barns or sheds.

Coastal towns such as Braintree feared attack at any minute. Militiamen went door-to-door to seek pewter for ammunition. Young John Quincy watched as Adams melted down her treasured spoons for musket balls. When an entire colonial regiment camped in the attic and barn one night, John Quincy joined their drill in the backyard the next morning.

"Our house has been . . . a scene of confusion," Adams wrote to John in Philadelphia. "[Y]ou can hardly imagine how we live." She knew she might have to flee if an attack came. John had said she could go to his brother's home inland: "In Case of real Danger . . . fly to the Woods with our Children," he wrote. Adams chose to stay in Braintree.

A little over a month after the battles of Lexington and Concord, England sent reinforcements to Boston. The redcoats were now 8,000 strong. Delegates in the Continental Congress knew they needed a real army, not just a militia, to oppose the British. John Adams nominated George Washington to be commander of the Continental

55

army. Washington was unanimously approved and took on a monumental task.

## The Battle of Bunker Hill

By late spring 1775, colonists had learned that the British planned to cross the harbor from Boston to seize Charlestown—the site of the Massachusetts militia's main camp. Overnight on June 16, the Patriots—the colonists who supported the formation of a new nation—fortified Breed's Hill at the foot of Bunker Hill near Charlestown. Before dawn, when the British spotted the trenches, their ships let loose a barrage of cannon fire.

British warships were equipped with 18-pound cannons—named for the size of the cannonballs they shot. The big guns fired flaming cannonballs at Charlestown, which set fields and homes on fire. An assault by British soldiers followed the naval barrage. They attacked in waves. The Patriots, low on musket balls and gunpowder, were ordered to hold their fire against the oncoming British soldiers until they could "see the whites of their eyes."

Not wasting a shot, the Patriots repelled two infantry charges at Breed's Hill, as they took cover behind hay bales. By the third advance, however, the Americans were out of ammunition. British bayonets were too much for the clubs and fists of the Patriots. The British took Breed's Hill.

When the battle was over, 140 Patriots had been killed. More than 200 British had died, and 800

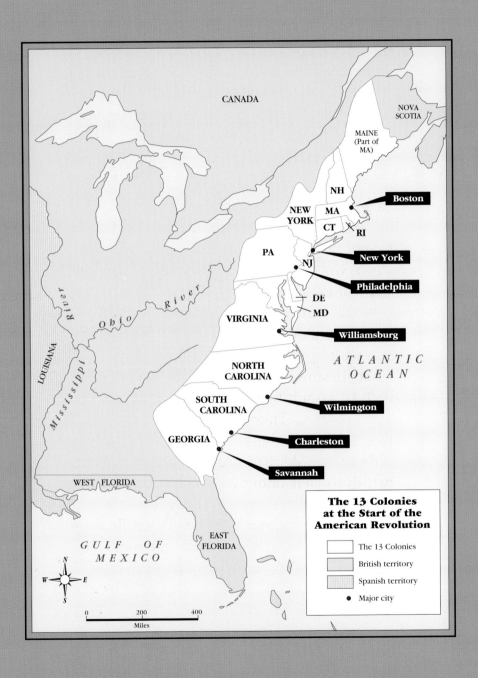

CANADA

NOVA SCOTIA

MAINE (Part of MA)

NH

NEW YORK

MA

CT

RI

**Boston**

PA

NJ

**New York**

**Philadelphia**

DE

MD

VIRGINIA

**Williamsburg**

ATLANTIC OCEAN

NORTH CAROLINA

SOUTH CAROLINA

**Wilmington**

GEORGIA

**Charleston**

**Savannah**

Ohio River

Mississippi River

LOUISIANA

WEST FLORIDA

EAST FLORIDA

GULF OF MEXICO

N
W    E
S

0        200        400
Miles

### The 13 Colonies at the Start of the American Revolution

| | The 13 Colonies |
| | British territory |
| | Spanish territory |
| ● | Major city |

more were wounded. Most of those killed had been British officers, a serious loss to the military structure. Though the British had taken the hill, the Patriot militia was encouraged. Upon hearing news of the Patriots' bravery at the misnamed Battle of Bunker Hill, Washington said, "The country is safe."

Dr. Joseph Warren, the Adamses' close friend, had been killed in the battle. Grief-stricken, Abigail told John about it in a letter, then had to lay down her pen with a "bursting Heart." A week later, she wrote to her husband of her fears that the British would advance to the outlying towns. "We live in continual Expectation of Hostilities," she wrote. John wrote back to bolster her courage: "You sustain with so much Fortitude, the Shocks and Terrors of the Times. You are really brave, my dear, you are an Heroine."

## Mrs. Delegate

If there had ever been any hope that an all-out battle for liberty could be avoided, that "decisive Day"—as Abigail Adams called the Battle of Bunker Hill—had made the truth plain. In England, King George III issued a Proclamation of Rebellion, which acknowledged the colonies were in revolt. Two weeks later, Washington arrived in Boston to review his Continental army.

From Boston, Washington sent American troops to invade Canada, which the British owned. He hoped to prevent a British invasion from the north.

That mission failed, but Fort Ticonderoga, a strategic ammunition depot in northern New York, was captured. The Patriots gained several large cannons and a huge gunpowder supply in the victory.

In Philadelphia, some congressional delegates—people loyal to the Crown, known as Tories—still hoped to settle differences with England. Those who supported the revolutionary cause, however, moved from a desire to settle grievances to a push for total independence.

Throughout the summer, John received news from Abigail of the dire circumstances in Boston. "There is a Lady at the Foot of Pens Hill," he wrote in his journal, "who obliges me with clearer and fuller Intelligence, than I can get from a whole Committee of Gentlemen." He grew convinced that two things were now vitally important—an American navy and a document that would declare independence.

In Philadelphia, delegates at the State House held secret sessions to guard against British spies.

The Second Continental Congress met in Carpenter's Hall.

John's letters home were often intercepted, so he took pains to have them delivered by people he could trust. One such messenger was none other than Washington, who traveled from Philadelphia to Boston after his appointment. After their meeting, Abigail Adams described him: "Dignity with ease, the Gentleman and Soldier look agreeably blended in him. Modesty marks every line and feature of his face."

As the wife of a delegate, Adams fulfilled social obligations by providing hospitality to generals and John's other associates when they arrived in Boston. She dined with the famous inventor and patriot Benjamin Franklin. Around Boston, she became known as Mrs. Delegate. "Why should we not assume your titles when we give you up our names?" she wrote to her husband.

Adams gracefully managed her public profile, but she missed her husband terribly and longed for personal expressions from John—"some sentimental Effusions of the heart," she called them. John's time, however, was not his own. When Congress recessed at the end of the summer, he went directly to a meeting of the Massachusetts legislature. He visited his family on weekends, then spent only three short weeks at home before he returned to Philadelphia.

## Disease and Difficulties

In the autumn of 1775, it was not redcoats but disease that brought fear to the Adams household.

60

An epidemic of dysentery swept through Braintree and Weymouth. Adams and young Tommy caught it, but recovered. A servant, John's brother, and Adams's mother, all died of the intestinal disease.

Adams mourned that fall. She was exhausted from illness and the burdens of maintaining the farm. After Thanksgiving, she suffered from jaundice and rheumatism. Snow and cold swirled around the farmhouse and ruined hundreds of barrels of apples. Adams battled depression and briefly regretted the "sacrifice" her husband's constant absence forced her to make.

At the same time, however, she realized the "ten thousand Difficulties" that confronted John and the other delegates as they formed a new government. When he returned home for Christmas, John saw that illness had taken a toll on Adams. They discussed whether John should resign from Congress. In the end, their sense of public duty surmounted personal trials, and John continued his service.

## Turning the Tide

In January 1776, back in Philadelphia, John sent his wife a copy of a newly published pamphlet called *Common Sense*, written by Thomas Paine. Abigail found the work inspiring, and urged John not to "hesitate one moment at adopting its sentiments." The widely read work lifted the idea of independence beyond theory and debate, and helped sway public opinion in favor of a complete

61

Thomas Paine came to Philadelphia from England in 1774.

break from England. John, who agreed with the pamphlet, felt it did not go far enough. He quickly wrote and published an anonymous reply, *Thoughts on Government.*

At the end of February 1776, the British Parliament denounced as traitors any Americans who did not support Crown rule and threatened to hang them. In Boston, Washington surveyed the situation. In order to retake the city, he would need more powerful artillery. He ordered huge cannons brought overland from Fort Ticonderoga. In early March, he laid siege to the city. He positioned the big guns on the hills of Dorchester Heights, and aimed them at the British below. Adams wrote to her husband that she could hear cannon fire for days.

British General William Howe, who had taken over for Thomas Gage, saw that the situation was hopeless. He boarded his men onto ships after they took whatever they could in raids. The British sailed out of Boston Harbor on March 17.

Adams witnessed what she called a "Forrest" of ships leaving. Many Americans celebrated the evacuation. Adams, however, had a sense of foreboding. "Many people are elated with their quitting Boston," she wrote. "I confess I do not feel so, tis only lifting the burden from one shoulder to the other which perhaps is less able or less willing to support."

William Howe commanded British forces in the colonies until 1777.

In the meantime, the silencing of the cannons did bring some relief. As the spring of 1776 approached, Adams breathed easier than she had the year before. "Now we feel as if we might sit under our own vine and eat the good of the land," she wrote. "I think the Sun looks brighter, the Birds sing more melodiously, and Nature puts on a more chearfull countance. We feel a temporary peace."

The peace was indeed temporary. The British had sailed north to Nova Scotia on the eastern coast of Canada, and no one was sure what their next step would be.

63

★

In 1776, the American ship *Alfred*, under Captain John Paul Jones, captured eight British merchant ships.

★

# "Remember the Ladies"

In the latter half of 1776, the fighting in the war began to move southward towards New York and New Jersey. It seemed that the British had given up on the idea of retaining control over New England. In truth, the colonies in warmer climates offered more to the Crown. With better weather, more land, and farms that grew cash crops, colonies from New Jersey southward became the focus of British military strategy.

With a respite from conflict, Adams thought and wrote about the deeper meaning of liberty. She wondered how independence would affect women. As the wife of a lawyer, she knew that their current legal status left women dependent on husbands or fathers. Women had no financial share in the property they labored to maintain. They had no redress in court if they were abused. Most alarming to Adams, women had no legal authority over the education of their children.

As the Continental Congress shaped a new nation, Adams wrote John one of her best-known letters, in which she asked him to include women in the Congress's plans:

> *Remember the Ladies, and be more generous and favourable to them than your ancestors. Do not put such unlimited power into the hands of the Husbands. Remember all Men*

64

*would be tyrants if they could . . . . Why then, not put it out of the power of the vicious and the Lawless to use us with cruelty and indignity . . . . Men of Sense in all ages abhor those customs which treat us only as the vassals of your Sex. Regard us then as Beings placed by providence under your protection and in imitation of the Supreem Being make use of that power only for our happiness.*

Adams did not ask for political equality or the right to vote. That would have been more progressive than her century could bear. She simply wanted legal rights for women. John laughed at her request, calling her "saucy." He wrote that Congress would not repeal masculine systems. Then, softening, he told his wife that the established systems were really only theory. In actuality, he replied in a jovial manner, men were subject to women and were masters in name only.

Adams was not pleased that John did not take her seriously. "I can not say that I think you very generous to the Ladies," she wrote, "for whilst you are proclaiming peace and good will to Men, Emancipating all Nations, you insist upon retaining an absolute power over Wives."

Later, she wrote again to ask John for a "more liberal plan" for education. Young girls were not as well educated as boys, if they were educated at all. "If we mean to have Heroes, Statesmen and Philosophers, we should have learned women," she wrote.

65

# Ladies to Remember

Abigail Adams was only one woman who played a key role in the American Revolution. Countless women worked behind battle lines to cart food and supplies into camps, cook and wash for the troops, tend to wounded soldiers, sew uniforms, and keep children safe. Many memorable Patriot women played a leading part in the war for independence.

**Penelope Barker**—In North Carolina in 1774, one woman decided to hold a tea party of her own—but there was no tea served. Barker gathered 51 women in her home and read them her own declaration: "We women have taken too long to let our voices be heard," she said. She asked all of them not to drink tea or wear garments made from English cloth. Every one of the women signed the declaration. This act inspired women all over the colonies to take a similar stand.

**Elizabeth Burgin**—American prisoners of war were often held in filthy, cramped British ships. In New York Harbor, many were starved or beaten. Burgin was allowed to row out to take the prisoners food, yet she wished she could do more. When a Patriot asked her to help smuggle men off the ships, she alerted the prisoners to the plan and helped them escape. With a price on her head, she was chased up the East Coast, but she was never caught. In return for her service, Burgin was granted a military pension.

**Lydia Darragh**—As the British schemed to seize Philadelphia in December 1777, they held a meeting one night at the home of Lydia Darragh. In the middle of the night, she overheard their plan to attack George Washington's troops in Whitemarsh. The next day, she walked halfway to the Patriot camp and delivered the news to two soldiers. Because of her message, the British lost the battle.

They suspected that Darragh had worked as a spy against them, but they could never prove it.

**Sybil Ludington**—Sybil was only 16 years old, but she saved her town of Fredricksburg, New York, and nearby villages. After the British burned and raided Danbury, Connecticut, a Patriot warned Sybil's father that the redcoats were on their way. Because the rider was exhausted, Sybil took over the job of alerting the militia. She rode half the night, calling men to arms. They assembled and successfully repelled the British. Sybil became known as the female Paul Revere.

**Molly Pitcher** also known as Mary Ludwig Hays—In June 1778, the Continental army marched to Monmouth, New Jersey, to engage a British force. On a brutally hot, humid day, Molly carried pitchers of water for soldiers to drink and for gunners to pour on the over-heated barrels of their cannons. "Molly bring a pitcher!" the men yelled. "Molly! Pitcher!" Suddenly, her husband, a gunner, was shot at his cannon. Molly tended to his wounds, then took over his job as a gunner. George

Molly Pitcher became famous for her bravery at the Battle of Monmouth.

Washington made Molly a sergeant in the army for her bravery.

**Deborah Sampson**—Some women's passion for liberty was so intense, they felt compelled to take up arms. Sampson was determined to join the Continental army. She cut her hair, bound her chest, donned a man's uniform, and enlisted in a Massachusetts regiment under her brother's name. For 18 long months, she fought side-by-side with other soldiers, painstakingly hiding her secret. It was not until she fell ill with a fever that a doctor discovered Sampson was a woman. She earned an honorable discharge and an army pension.

Although her pleas brought few results at the time, Adams had introduced a woman's voice into the affairs of men. In doing so, she opened a dialogue for progress in women's rights in later generations.

## Declaring Independence

Although the British had left Boston, Adams feared their return. She wondered if Congress had forgotten her city. "Two months have elapsed since the evacuation of Boston," she wrote to John, "and very little has been done in that time to secure it, or the Harbour from future invasion.... A Government of more Stability is much wanted in this colony, and they [colonists] are ready to receive it from the Hands of the Congress."

The delegates were making progress in Philadelphia. Even though many Americans had remained loyal to England, Thomas Paine's pamphlet *Common Sense* had helped sway opinion in the south to the revolutionary cause. On June 7, 1776, Virginia delegate Richard Henry Lee made a motion to the Continental Congress to vote for complete independence. He called on the delegates to dissolve political ties to the British Crown.

A committee quickly formed to draft a declaration. John Adams was on the committee. So were John Hancock and Benjamin Franklin. Thomas Jefferson, a young Virginian about Abigail's age with a flair for words, was chosen to write the draft. In little more than two weeks, working with the committee, Jefferson composed one of the most famous political documents ever written, the Declaration of Independence.

Not all delegates agreed that the declaration should be adopted. Some felt that America was ill-prepared to fight an all-out war. Others feared a costly loss of human

Benjamin Franklin, John Adams, Thomas Jefferson, and two other delegates formed the committee that drafted the Declaration of Independence.

life and destruction of the cities. John Adams, however, spoke eloquently in support of the split with England. Finally, the vote was taken, and on July 2, 1776, the declaration was approved. Adams called it the "Day of Deliverance."

Printed copies were distributed almost immediately throughout the colonies. As the stirring words were read aloud, they created a passion for liberty in many Americans. Now that independence had been declared, it had to be won.

# Chapter 4

## WAR AND DIPLOMACY

The news that Congress had declared independence was less important to many Bostonians than the smallpox epidemic that spread through the city in the summer of 1776. Abigail Adams took her four children to her uncle Isaac's home to be inoculated. People who went through the inoculation ordeal were infected with pus from one of the pox that caused the disease, and confined until a mild case of the disease developed. The problem was that the inoculation was inexact. Some people, including Adams, received much more than a mild case. Adams's eyes became so inflamed, she could not write to John for nearly a month. Nabby's inoculation gave her so many pox that her face was scarred for life. Little Charles nearly died.

OPPOSITE: In August 1776, a force of more than 30,000 British soldiers landed in Long Island, New York.

Adams was well enough at one point to attend a public reading of the Declaration of Independence. People cheered as the British king's coat of arms was taken down from the State House and burned in the streets.

In New York, the news of independence was not celebrated as joyfully. While the Continental Congress took its historic vote to sever ties with the Crown, the British fleet had sailed into New York Harbor. Most New Yorkers were Loyalist Tories. In fact, 6,000 more New Yorkers had enlisted in the king's army than in the Continental army. Soon, 500 ships were in the city, loaded with regular troops, hired soldiers from Germany (known as Hessians), and Scottish warriors.

During the last half of 1776, the British army drove George Washington's troops out of Manhattan and across the Hudson River into New Jersey. By December 1776, the Continentals had retreated across the Delaware River, into Pennsylvania. Then, in one of the great maneuvers of the war, Washington rallied his weary men for a victory in Trenton, New Jersey, on December 26 and one in nearby Princeton on January 2, 1777.

## Loss at Home

While the fighting took place in New Jersey toward the end of 1776, John returned to Braintree to spend time with his wife and children. He hoped his homecoming would be for good, but he was reelected to attend the next session of Congress.

The decision whether to go was heartrending, because Abigail was pregnant again. Once again, public duty won out over private happiness. John departed, this time for Baltimore, because Congress had moved south in fear of a British attack in Philadelphia.

It was an especially hard winter for Abigail Adams. Food and supply shortages drove up prices. Few men were available for labor—most were away fighting. By the end of her pregnancy, when she was nearly too big to walk, there were rumors of a new British attack on Massachusetts. If it came, Adams did not know how she would move her family to safety. Then she began to feel ill. After a difficult delivery in July 1777, a baby girl, who Adams named Elizabeth, was stillborn. The tragedy grieved the whole family. John wrote, "Never in my whole Life, was my Heart affected with such Emotions."

★

In 1777, Thomas Paine was secretary to a newly created foreign affairs committee of the Continental Congress in Philadelphia.

★

Both he and Adams were grateful that Abigail had not died in childbirth, which was not unusual at that time. Adams recovered quickly, but the loss took its toll on her. She lamented her husband's absence as a "sacrifice" and "great misfortune."

John felt like a "miserable Exile from every Thing that is agreeable to me." Still, he could not get away. Because he was chairman of the Board of War and Ordnance, his presence at Congress was essential, especially when General Howe seized Philadelphia in September 1777.

73

## A Turning Point

In October 1777, a triumph by the Continental army at Saratoga, New York, became the turning point of the war. The Crown's plan to cut America in two at the Hudson River had failed. France, now convinced that the Americans could win the war, agreed to send desperately needed soldiers, supplies, and money.

The victory that gave Americans cause to rejoice presented Abigail Adams with a new conflict. Now that France was willing to support America, the former colonies needed to negotiate an alliance. Congress elected John as a commissioner to assist Benjamin Franklin, who was already in France.

Adams was aware of the honor this position bestowed on her husband, but she knew it also presented real danger. Crossing the ocean in the winter was dangerous enough in peacetime. In wartime, a ship could easily be captured by the powerful British navy and John could be imprisoned or executed. Adams longed to have him at home. She felt she could not face another winter alone, and the children desperately missed their father.

The dangers also bothered John, but he felt that the fate of his country hung in the balance. The success of the war depended on a firm alliance with France. Without French aid, John feared, everything he had worked for might fail. John told Abigail he would stay home if she asked him. She did not.

## An Ocean Apart

John took his oldest son John Quincy with him to France in early 1778. The bright ten-year-old could help his father with clerical work and could also study abroad.

The journey to Paris lasted months. Storms raged at sea. Twice, British warships chased and nearly seized the ship on which the Adamses were traveling. The ship finally arrived safely in April 1778, but Adams did not receive John's letters until June. For months, she did not know if her husband and son were dead or alive.

For the next year and a half, Adams was depressed and lonely. Nabby was at school in Boston. Hoping to learn more about her husband's activities, Adams corresponded with two of his associates in Philadelphia, John Thaxter and James Lovell.

John Adams found France both delightful and difficult. He wrote to Abigail that he thought the women were well-educated. He had problems, however, because he knew little of the French language and court customs. His worst problems involved his responsibilities as a delegate. He thought his delegation wasted money. Because communications from Congress took months, the delegates had little direction. To make matter worse, the other two American commissioners, Benjamin Franklin and Arthur Lee, were at odds. John had to serve as a mediator. In September 1778, Congress appointed Franklin as sole minister, and John was able to return home.

Benjamin Franklin (left) was one of the most popular men in Paris, France, where he served as an American minister during the Revolution.

John and Abigail's reunion did much to restore their happiness, but their contented life was short-lived. In October, John was asked to return to France. Because he felt duty-bound to help his country, and also because he wanted a chance to be more effective than on his last mission, John accepted the job.

The constant sacrifice was hard for Adams, but when John left—this time with his two oldest sons,

John Quincy and Charles—she was determined to adjust, to learn new skills, and to use the opportunity to grow. She rented out the farm to a manager and tried her hand at trade.

When John arrived in Europe, he began to send his wife goods for the American market—handkerchiefs, glassware, cloth, lace, ribbons, porcelain, and tea. Adams sold these to make a small income. Soon, she began to order directly from merchants in Holland, France, and Spain. With some of the income, she made investments for the future. At the same time, she kept in touch with her husband and sent him news of the war.

## War Winds Down

By 1781, the Revolution was being fought mainly in the south. In mid-October, more than 15,000 American and French troops, supported by a French fleet, had trapped British general Charles Cornwallis on the York River in eastern Virginia. Cornwallis surrendered at Yorktown, in the last real battle of the war. More than one-third of the British army was captive.

The formal peace treaty that ended the war was not signed until 15 months after Yorktown. John was a key member of the team that negotiated the treaty. It was a difficult process. John suspected—correctly—that France wanted too much control over America. He insisted that America formulate a separate set of agreements with England before France joined the negotiation.

Cornwallis surrendered at Yorktown after more than a week of artillery bombardment from American and French forces.

The years from 1781 to 1783 were the most trying of the many times that Abigail Adams had been left home. She received few letters from her husband and sons for an entire year. John had allowed John Quincy, now 14, to travel to Russia as secretary to the American minister. Charles had been sent back to Massachusetts, but it took five months for him to arrive. When Charles told her that John had been ill during his time abroad, Abigail felt helpless. She wrote of a "dejection of spirits" that she could not overcome. She even complained that she felt like a widow. In fact,

Abigail and John had spent eleven of the past twenty years apart.

John feared that Congress, France, and the British Parliament would take years to approve a final peace treaty. He could not decide whether to resign or stay at his post. Neither he nor Abigail could endure the separation much longer. Abigail's father had recently died, and she felt more alone than ever. The Adams children were nearly grown. If John would not come home, Abigail must join him in Europe.

At the end of 1783, when the Treaty of Paris was finally signed, Congress gave John a commission to negotiate a treaty of trade and commerce with Great Britain. He would work in Paris with Benjamin Franklin and Thomas Jefferson. John immediately sent for Abigail. Over the winter, she made arrangements for the care of her children, the farmhouse, and finances.

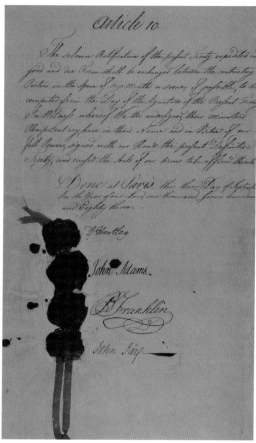

The Treaty of Paris, signed by John Adams and other Americans, officially ended the Revolution.

79

## Foreigner in France

After four years apart, Abigail and John were finally reunited in London in June 1783. Together with Nabby and John Quincy, they spent a few weeks there before they joined the other commissioners in Paris. Adams was amazed at the size of London compared to Boston. She was impressed with the grand architecture of St. James's Palace, St. Paul's Cathedral, Westminster Abbey, and the beautiful townhouses and squares. She was dismayed, however, at the high prices and all the attention paid to appearing "fashionable."

The family soon moved on to France. The Adamses rented a mansion in the French suburb of Auteuil, close to Passy, where Franklin lived. Abigail Adams had difficulty adjusting to her new surroundings. Although she appreciated the beauty of Notre Dame Cathedral and the Palais de Justice, she thought Paris was crowded and dirty. She had gone from living in a small farmhouse in Braintree to a 30-room mansion.

Now that Adams was the wife of a foreign minister and in the public eye, people expected her and her husband to conform to a certain standard of living. The Adamses had to attend parties and entertain guests. When they went out, it had to be in a gilded carriage. Although homespun clothing had served the family well in America, they now were expected to dress in fashion. Congress, however, had not granted John enough salary to

Abigail Adams found it difficult to adjust to the fashionable life of Paris.

keep up such a lifestyle. French custom required Adams to hire and pay for eight servants, who would barely do their chores because they had little respect for the Americans.

By far, Adams's greatest pleasure was to have the family together every day to dine, converse, and walk in the park. Adams also had a small reading room, adjoining her bedchamber, where she wrote letters to her sisters and friends at home while she looked out over the gardens.

One visitor who spent much time with the Adamses was Thomas Jefferson. His wife had died recently, and he was left to raise three young daughters. This charming southern gentleman—tall, handsome, intelligent, and witty—was always welcome at the Adams home. Abigail Adams spent many hours conversing with him. She later wrote, "He is one of the choice ones of the earth."

## Life in London

In May 1785, Congress appointed John to serve as the first American minister to England. The Adamses both feared how they would be treated by their recent enemies in England, but John could not turn down such a prominent post.

The Adamses moved to London and rented a townhouse in Grosvenor Square. Soon, they were presented formally to King George III and Queen

London was one of the wealthiest cities in the world in the 1700s.

Charlotte. After the Adamses waited for four hours for the royal couple to make their way around a huge circle of court visitors, the king finally greeted them politely.

Life in England did have a positive side. Abigail Adams loved seeing Shakespeare's plays performed. She attended concerts and lectures, and made

83

friends with some people who supported the Americans. She also met the historian Catherine Macaulay, whose work she had long admired.

When John was busy, Adams occasionally traveled with Nabby to the countryside. Nabby had been engaged to be married in Massachusetts, but then broke the engagement while abroad. As a result, she had been sullen much of the time in Europe. In England, a new young man caught her eye—Colonel William Smith—the secretary to the American delegation. He courted Nabby, and they were married in June 1786. By the next April, Adams had a grandson.

Because she missed Jefferson's company, Adams began to correspond with him. The two had similar views on most political issues. They expressed sharply different opinions, however, when a farmer's rebellion broke out in America. Called Shays's Rebellion after one of the leaders, the episode roused Adams's anger. She and Jefferson disagreed about the violent outbreak that arose over the new U.S. government's tax and money policies.

Overseas, Abigail and John saw Shays's Rebellion as an attempt at mob rule, something they had always disdained. They were deeply distressed that Americans would turn against one another. Jefferson, however, applauded the farmers. He wrote to Abigail that he valued the spirit of resistance to government. "I like a little rebellion now and then," he said.

# Looking Homeward

In the summer of 1787, a convention was held in America to write a new constitution. Because John could not be there, he put his thoughts into a treatise called *A Defense of the Constitutions of Government of the United States of America.* John was in favor of a strong central government, within a framework of democracy. Many people who read the piece, however, believed that John really wanted a monarchy.

In April 1788, the Adamses set sail for home. The time abroad had "more attached me to America," Abigail wrote. "Retiring to our own little farm feeding my poultry and improving my garden has more charms for my fancy, than residing at the court of Saint James."

# Chapter 5

## "SPLENDID MISERY"

T he ship that carried Abigail and John Adams from Europe landed in Massachusetts in June 1788. The docks were lined with thousands of cheering well-wishers. Cannons boomed and church bells pealed to herald the ambassador's joyous return. Governor John Hancock whisked the Adamses away in his coach for a lavish reception at his mansion. Abigail never cared for Hancock's showy style, but she was gracious.

OPPOSITE: Washington D.C. was little more than a country village in 1800.

87

During the Adams's long absence, Abigail arranged for her uncle to purchase a larger home for when she and John returned to Braintree. After staying for a few days with Hancock, they proceeded quietly to their new home.

Abigail Adams had admired the new house since she was young. Now that she had lived in spacious European quarters, however, it seemed as small as a "wren's nest." To make matters worse, the grounds were overgrown. Abigail and John had to work hard to clean up the gardens and prepare the house.

It was one of the happiest summers in Adams's long life. Her younger sons were at home, John Quincy worked nearby, and John's mother was still in Braintree. Nabby and her new family had arrived safely in New York, and Adams's beloved sister Mary lived close enough to visit almost every day. John fittingly named their new estate "Peacefield."

## Second Lady

The tranquil time at Peacefield proved to be short-lived. Elections for the first president and vice president of the United States were held in November 1788. Most Americans expected George Washington to be elected president. Political associates urged John to run for vice president. He felt he was "too honest" to hold public office, but said he would welcome the recognition.

In the first use of the electoral college under the new Constitution, citizens voted on electors to

New York City was the nation's first capital in 1789.

represent them, then the electors cast votes for their preferred candidate for president. There was no running mate in the first presidential elections. All votes were cast for the office of president. The man who received the second-most votes became vice president. In 1788, John Adams was that man.

In the spring of 1789, Adams proceeded to New York City, the first capital of the United States. He was officially inaugurated at Federal Hall and gave a speech to the Senate. On April 30, George Washington, who had been elected unanimously, was inaugurated as the first president. Jefferson was appointed secretary of state.

Abigail Adams stayed behind in Massachusetts to finish the work at Peacefield. John rented an unfurnished house and 30 acres high on a hill above the Hudson River in Richmond Heights. He was eager for Adams to crate up the furniture and join him.

In June 1789, Abigail brought Charles and her niece Louisa with her to New York. Thomas, Nabby, and her sons soon joined them. Adams loved the view from the hill, the gardens, and the birds.

Thrown into the limelight of politics, however, Adams found herself required to entertain every day of the week. It was proper for the vice president's wife—the second lady— to hold open houses, teas, dinners, and to return every visit. First Lady Martha Washington became Adams's trusted friend and a model of required etiquette. Adams could also draw on her own years of practice in England and France.

## Poor Health

In September 1790, John returned to Braintree for a rest while Adams stayed in New York. Suddenly, illness struck. Nabby's baby came down with smallpox, and Adams suffered from rheumatism and fever. Even George Washington nearly died from illness, but recovered.

While Adams regained her health, she read Noah Webster's newly published book on American spelling. Because she had not been formally schooled, she had always felt self-conscious about her poor punctuation, grammar, and spelling. She welcomed Webster's system.

In November 1790, the seat of federal government moved to Philadelphia. Though she hated to leave her home on the hill, once again Adams packed her furniture. Before she could move, she was stricken with malaria. When she was able to make the trip, the Adamses moved to a house in Philadelphia that had not been used for four years and needed constant work.

## Political Factions

While the Adamses had been abroad, another revolution—this one political—had been waged over the new Constitution. Americans were deeply divided over whether the states or the federal government should have more rights, and how much power the federal government should have. John and Abigail were on the side of Federalism, which supported a strong national government. Their position made them unpopular with many people who thought a strong federal government was too much like royalty. The Adamses' views even put them in direct conflict with former friends. The long relationship between Abigail Adams and Mercy Otis Warren was broken when the Warrens campaigned against the Constitution. Adams thought Warren was "gravely misled."

★

In 1790, Cornwallis was the governor-general of the British colony of India.

★

A rift also developed in the Adamses' relationship with Thomas Jefferson. As a Republican, Jefferson supported states' rights. The Republicans were against strong federal government. Some Republicans claimed that John Adams favored monarchy. When Thomas Paine published a document called *The Rights of Man*, denouncing the English constitution and Parliament, Jefferson supported it. He said Paine's paper countered political "heresies" that were circulating—a reference to John Adams's views.

John felt his views were grossly misinterpreted. As a Federalist, he did believe that people from the educated upper classes were the most fit to rule, but he was strongly in favor of a balance of power in government. Abigail was so angered at Jefferson's remarks that she did not write to him for years. Under a pen name, John Quincy defended his father in the press, but a political rivalry between the Adamses and Jefferson was born.

Despite the controversy, John was reelected to the vice presidency in 1792. Because his salary was so small, it was cheaper for the family to live in Massachusetts than to rent a home in Philadelphia. Besides, traveling between Massachusetts and Pennsylvania had exhausted Abigail. She decided that she would stay at Peacefield during John's second term as vice president.

By 1793, Europe was in turmoil and the United States was in danger of being drawn into it. A revolution was tearing France apart. The king and many others were beheaded. Christianity was abolished in France, and Abigail called the conditions there a "moral earthquake." At the same time, England was on the verge of going to war with France—and with America too, since the alliance John had worked to create was still in effect.

Washington and the Federalists claimed a neutral position with France in 1795. This angered

French peasants stormed the Bastille in 1793 to begin the bloody French Revolution.

Jefferson and the Republicans, who supported the French revolutionaries. The United States was split between the two factions, which opposed each other like political parties. When Washington announced that he would not seek a third term as president in 1796, the highest post in the land was available.

## First Lady

After he asked Abigail Adams whether he should run for president and received her approval, John decided to enter the race against his now-rival, Thomas Jefferson. John won the electoral college by the thin margin of 3 votes. Jefferson became vice president. For the first time, two men of different political views became the country's top leaders.

93

Thomas Jefferson and the Adamses had serious political disagreements in the 1790s.

Much to the new president's regret, Abigail Adams was in Massachusetts waiting for winter to end during his inauguration on March 4, 1797. Because he knew he and his new vice president were divided in political philosophy, John desperately craved his wife's support. He wrote to her, "I cannot live without you . . . I never wanted [needed] your advice and assistance more in my life. . . . The times are critical and dangerous, and I must have you here to assist me. I can do nothing without you."

At the end of April, Abigail Adams began the long journey to Philadelphia. A few miles outside the city, John's carriage approached hers. He had ridden out to meet her. With Adams now by his side, he was filled with hope and courage.

Being the first lady required Adams to supervise a large and complex staff. She planned menus and held large state dinners. Some days she entertained as many as 60 guests in a few hours. A friend called her position "splendid misery."

Always knowledgeable about political activity, Adams was a valued adviser to her husband. She often wrote letters to support the president's views and respond to criticism of him in the press.

## Alien and Sedition Acts

As a Federalist, Adams remained neutral on matters that related to France. The French resented this, and the French navy began to attack American ships. By the fall of 1797, the United States was on the verge of war. To defend the nation, Adams saw to it that a department of the navy was created and that 24 new warships were built. In the spring of 1798, John Adams was briefly considered a hero for avoiding war.

Soon, however, the press renewed its attacks on the president's policies. Abigail believed the newspapers printed lies—especially those papers published by people sympathetic with France. The articles became so extreme in their charges that the Adamses and some of their supporters were convinced that French agitators were sneaking into the country to destroy America. Abigail and John believed in freedom of speech and a free press, but they also felt that newspapers had a responsibility to print the truth.

As a result of these events, Congress, with the president's approval, passed the Alien and Sedition Acts in 1798. These new laws allowed for the arrest of newspaper editors who published sedition, or slander, and remarks that impeded the government. The alien laws made it harder for foreigners to become citizens and deported those found guilty of promoting dissent or rebellion.

Many people immediately condemned these laws. The harsh penalties the laws imposed hurt

95

John's reputation. Republicans said the laws were a political attempt to stifle any opposition, and Jefferson felt the laws were unconstitutional. The controversial laws were repealed in 1801.

## Family Matters

During the summer of 1798, Abigail Adams suffered a relapse of malaria at Peacefield. Confined to her bed for three months, she was near death. By fall, she still was not strong enough to go to Philadelphia. John returned to the capital alone.

When Adams finally recovered, she turned her attention to her family. Nabby now had three children, and over the years, her husband, William Smith, had barely supported his family. One or another of the children often lived with Adams, and she arranged for their education.

★

In 1798, Thomas Paine lived in Paris after his release from a French prison where he had been confined during that nation's revolution.

★

John Quincy had served under President Washington as ambassador to Holland, and now he was abroad again, serving as the minister to Prussia. He had left his financial affairs for his younger brother to manage. When Charles mismanaged John Quincy's money, Adams had to take over. Charles worried Adams. Depression and alcoholism were ruining him.

In the fall of 1799, Adams was well enough to return to Philadelphia. She arrived in a flurry of social activity. The capital would soon be moving to the new "Federal City" of Washington, D.C. Until then, Adams used her renewed energy to entertain.

The country was gearing up for a new presidential election. John was criticized by both the Jeffersonian Republicans and extremists within his own Federalist party, such as Alexander Hamilton. Hamilton wanted war with France, but John was committed to diplomacy. He delivered an influential speech to Congress in December 1799 that advocated peace and trade.

John Adams became president in 1797.

## In the Federal City

George Washington died just before Christmas 1799, marking the end of a century as well as the end of an era. As 1800 dawned, it was clear that the vice president, Jefferson, would run against the president, Adams, in the presidential election. Hamilton wrote a paper that called Adams eccentric, egotistical, weak, and angry. This split in the Federalist party only served to benefit Jefferson's campaign and hurt John's chances to win the election.

In the fall of 1800, Congress reconvened in Washington, D.C. John arrived before Abigail did and wrote to her of the new president's mansion, "I pray heaven to bestow the best of blessing on this house, and on all that shall hereafter inhabit it. May none but honest and wise men ever rule under

97

Abigail played
an important role
as first lady.

this roof." (Today, those words are carved in marble in the State Dining Room of the White House.)

On her way to join John in Washington, Abigail Adams stopped to look in on Charles. She found him near death. At the end of November, he died from liver and lung disease. While Charles's widow remained at home with her two youngest children, Adams brought his oldest daughter, Susanna, with her to Washington.

Washington, D.C., was a 10-mile clearing in the woods, with half-finished buildings on two hills. The President's House—known today as the White House—was damp and cold. Not one room was finished. Adams lit fires in every room to dry the plaster, and used the empty space in the conference room to hang laundry. The one saving grace was the house's view of the Potomac River.

In early December, the election tally was in. Jefferson had received eight more electoral votes than Adams, but Aaron Burr, who also ran, had tied with Jefferson. The decision was placed in the hands of the members of the House of Representatives, and they selected Jefferson after 36 votes, or ballots.

In one way, Abigail and John Adams were relieved at the election results. Both of them had been at the center of politics and public affairs for almost forty years. They were ready for a change.

## Final Years

Many of Abigail Adams's last years were filled with sadness. Within days of one another, her older sister, Mary, and Mary's husband, Richard, died. Adams's daughter Nabby had developed cancer. She survived surgery, only to find later that the disease had spread throughout her body. Her death in 1813 was almost too much for Abigail to bear.

The strain grew worse when Adams's younger sister, Elizabeth, died suddenly in 1815. Then, both Thomas and John Quincy lost infant daughters within a year of one another. Through it all, however, Peacefield was visited often by Adams's many grandchildren.

★
In 1805, Cornwallis died in India and was buried there.
★

In later years, Adams also renewed her correspondence with Mercy Warren and Thomas Jefferson, old friends she had lost during times of political controversy. In the fall of 1819, John Quincy visited with Adams one last time. Soon afterward, she contracted typhoid fever. Surrounded by friends and family who loved her, she passed away quietly on October 28, 1818, just before her 74th birthday.

Abigail Adams lived long enough to see her oldest son achieve many successes. John Quincy had been elected to the Senate in 1803. In 1809, he was appointed ambassador to Russia and served with the same sense of duty and sacrifice that his parents had always shown. Like his father, John Quincy was sent to Europe as a peace commissioner when the United States was involved in the War of 1812. After the peace treaty with England was signed in 1814, John Quincy was appointed ambassador to that country. In 1817, President James Monroe made him secretary of state. Abigail had been proud of John Quincy and these successes, but she did not get to witness his ultimate achievement. Following in his father's footsteps again, he was elected sixth president of the United States in 1824.

Abigail's death devastated John Adams. The two had been married for 54 years. He himself lived for another seven years. During that time, he managed to heal old wounds with Jefferson. They wrote letters to each other until their deaths, on the same day, July 4, 1826—exactly 50 years after the adoption of the Declaration of Independence they both helped to write.

Abigail Adams left behind a legacy of letters that was unrivaled by women of her day and for many generations after. She had struggled with illness most of her life. She suffered from arthritis, dysentery, and even diabetes. Even when rheumatism stiffened her hands and cold winters froze the ink in her pen, however, she continued to record her thoughts on politics, education for women, independence, slavery, and her family.

Adams's letters revealed the daily effects of war on the home front during the American Revolution. They also contain her reflections on the birth of a nation. Although she spent much of her adult life alone, she expressed constant support of her husband's public role and, in a unique way, helped to shape the United States of America.

## Glossary

**alien**  a foreign-born person

**Continental army**  the first U.S. Army under George Washington's command

**Continental Congress**  the first U.S. Congress, representing 13 colonies

**Electoral College**  a body of representatives who cast votes in presidential elections

**Federalist**  member of a group or party that supported a strong central government

**House of Burgesses**  a legislative body representing boroughs or towns in Virginia

**Patriot**  a colonial supporter of the fight for liberty during the American Revolution

**rebel**  a Patriot who rebelled against English rule and fought for liberty of the colonies

**redcoat**  a British soldier during the Revolution, who wore red-jacketed uniforms

**republican**  member of a group or party that supported states' rights; also called a Democratic-Republican

**sedition**  slander and other actions that promote rebellion or discontent

**Tory**  member of a group or party that was loyal to the British Crown

101

# For More Information

## Books

Akers, Charles W. *Abigail Adams: An American Woman.* Library of American Biography. Boston: Little, Brown and Company, 1980.

Bober, Natalie S. *Abigail Adams: Witness to a Revolution.* New York: Atheneum Books for Young Readers, 1995.

Levin, Phyllis Lee. *Abigail Adams: A Biography.* New York: St. Martin's Press, 1987.

Marrin, Albert. *The War for Independence.* New York: Atheneum, 1988.

Osborne, Angela. *Abigail Adams: Women's Rights Advocate.* American Women of Achievement. New York: Chelsea House, 1989.

Wagoner, Jean Brown. *Abigail Adams: Girl of Colonial Days.* New York: Aladdin Paperbacks, 1992.

## Web Sites

*Abigail Adams Historical Society*
*http://www.abigailadams.org/Abigail/abigail.html*
This site contains a biography of Abigail as well as links to her homestead, portraits, and special events.

*First Ladies of the United States*
*http://www.firstladies.org/ABIGAIL_ADAMS/FL.HTML*
This site has a link to the White House First Ladies biography, as well as other sources and bibliographies.

# Index

Gage, Thomas, 52, 62

Hamilton, Alexander, 97
Hancock, John, 36, 48, 52–54, 68,
    87–88
Harvard College, 12, 18, 20
Henry, Patrick, 45
Hessian soldiers, 72
House of Burgesses, 48
House of Representatives, 98
Howe, General William, 62, 73

Intolerable Acts, 43

Jefferson, Thomas, 68–69, 79, 82,
    84, 89, 91–94, 96–97, 99–100

King George III, 26–27, 43, 58, 82

Lee, Arthur, 75
Lee, Henry, 68
Lovell, James, 75
Ludington, Sybil, 67

Macauley, Catherine, 44–45, 84
Massachusetts Bay Colony, 12, 15
Massachusetts Committee of
    Correspondence, 44
Minutemen, 53
Monroe, James, 99
Mount Wollaston, 14
Nicholson, Mary, 18

Paine, Eunice, 18
Paine, Thomas, 61, 68, 91
Palmer, Polly, 18
Patriots, 56–59
Peacefield, 88–89, 92, 96, 99
Pitcher, Molly, 67
Preface, 4–7
Proclamation of Rebellion, 58

Puritans, 15

Quincy, grandmother, 13–14
Quincy, John, 14, 32

Redcoats, 8–9, 36, 38–39, 53–55,
    60, 67
Republicans, 91, 93, 97
Revere, Paul, 44, 53, 67

Sampson, Deborah, 67
Senate, 89, 99
Shay's Rebellion, 84
Smith, Betsy, 13
Smith, Colonel William, 84, 96
Smith, Elizabeth, 12–14, 21, 30, 61
Smith, Isaac and Elizabeth, 18, 27,
    34, 71
Smith, Isaac Jr., 18
Smith, Mary, 13, 18, 19–20
Smith, William, 12–13, 15, 21, 22, 79
Sons of Liberty, 30
Stamp Act, 28, 30, 31, 36
Sugar Act, 27

Thaxter, John, 75
The Rights of Man, 91
Thoughts on Government, 62
Tories, 59, 72
Townshend Acts, 32, 36
Treaty of Paris, 79
Trenton, Battle of, 72

War of 1812, 99
Warren, Dr. Joseph, 36-37, 44, 53, 58
Warren, Mercy, 43–44, 91, 99
Washington D.C., 96–98
Washington, George, 55–58, 60, 66,
    67, 72, 89–90, 92–93, 96–97
Washington, Martha, 90
White House, 98

104